Incorporating Student Performance Measures into Teacher Evaluation Systems

Jennifer L. Steele, Laura S. Hamilton,
Brian M. Stecher

Sponsored by the Center for American Progress

This work was sponsored by the Center for American Progress with support from the Bill and Melinda Gates Foundation. The research was conducted in RAND Education, a unit of the RAND Corporation.

Library of Congress Control Number: 2011927262

ISBN: 978-0-8330-5250-6

Published 2010 by the RAND Corporation
1776 Main Street, P.O. Box 2138, Santa Monica, CA 90407-2138
1200 South Hayes Street, Arlington, VA 22202-5050
4570 Fifth Avenue, Suite 600, Pittsburgh, PA 15213-2665
RAND URL: http://www.rand.org/
To order RAND documents or to obtain additional information, contact
Distribution Services: Telephone: (310) 451-7002;
Fax: (310) 451-6915; Email: order@rand.org

Preface

Research tells us that teachers vary enormously in their ability to improve students' performance on standardized tests but that many existing teacher evaluation and reward systems do not capture that variation. Armed with this knowledge and with improved access to longitudinal data systems linking teachers to students, reform-minded policymakers are increasingly attempting to base a portion of teachers' evaluations or pay on student achievement gains. However, systems that incorporate student achievement gains into teacher evaluations face at least two important challenges: generating valid estimates of teachers' contributions to student learning and including teachers who do not teach subjects or grades that are tested annually. This report summarizes how three districts and two states have already begun or are planning to address these challenges. In particular, the report focuses on what is and is not known about the quality of various student performance measures school systems are using and on how the systems are supplementing these measures with other teacher performance indicators.

This report should be of interest to educational policymakers and practitioners at the federal, state, and local levels and to families and communities interested in policy strategies for evaluating and improving teacher effectiveness.

The research was carried out by RAND Education, a unit of the RAND Corporation, on behalf of the Center for American Progress, with support from the Bill and Melinda Gates Foundation.

Contents

Tables

Summary

The Use of Student Achievement to Evaluate Teachers Is Drawing Increasing Policy Attention

In a growing effort to recognize and reward teachers for their contributions to students' learning, a number of states and districts are retooling their teacher evaluation systems to incorporate measures of student performance. This trend stems from evidence that teachers' evaluations and reward structures have not sufficiently distinguished teachers who are more effective at raising student achievement from those who are less effective (Toch & Rothman, 2008; Tucker, 1997; Weisberg et al., 2009). It has also likely been spurred by competitive federal grant programs, such as Race to the Top and the Teacher Incentive Fund, and by philanthropic efforts, such as the Bill and Melinda Gates Foundation's Empowering Effective Teachers Initiative, all of which encourage states and districts to enhance the way they recruit, evaluate, retain, develop, and reward teachers. Given strong empirical evidence that teachers are the most important school-based determinant of student achievement (Rivkin et al., 2005; Sanders & Horn, 1998; Sanders & Rivers, 1996), it seems increasingly imperative to many education advocates that teacher evaluations take account of teachers' effects on student learning (Chait & Miller, 2010; Gordon et al., 2006; Hershberg, 2005).

Meanwhile, improved longitudinal data systems and refinements to a class of statistical techniques known as *value-added models* have made it increasingly possible for educational systems to estimate teachers' impacts on student learning by holding constant a variety of student, school, and classroom characteristics. However, measuring teachers' performance based on their value-added estimates involves several challenges. First, despite recent advances in value-added modeling, in practice, most value-added systems have a number of limitations: The tests on which they are based tend to be incomplete measures of the constructs of interest, year-to-year scaling is often inadequate, and student-teacher links are generally incomplete—particularly for highly mobile students or in cases of team teaching (Baker et al., 2010; Corcoran, 2010; McCaffrey et al., 2003). Second, value-added estimates can be calculated only for teachers of subjects and grades that are tested at least annually, such as those administered under a state's accountability system. In most states, the tested grades and subjects are only those required by No Child Left Behind: math and reading in grades 3–8.

In light of these limitations, educational systems that are now attempting to incorporate student achievement gains into teacher evaluations face at least two important challenges: generating valid estimates of teachers' contributions to student learning and including teachers who do not teach subjects or grades that are tested annually. This report considers these challenges in terms of the kinds of student performance measures that educational systems might use to measure teachers' effectiveness in a variety of grades and subject areas.

Considerations in Choosing Student Performance Measures to Evaluate Teachers

The report argues that policymakers should take particular measurement considerations into account when using student achievement data to inform teacher evaluations. Such considerations include score *reliability*, or the extent to which scores on an assessment are consistent over repeated measurements and are free of errors of measurement (AERA, APA, & NCME, 1999). We describe three reliability considerations in particular: the internal consistency of student assessment scores, the consistency of ratings among individuals scoring the assessments, and the consistency of teachers' value-added estimates generated from student assessment scores.

Policymakers should also consider evidence about the *validity* of inferences drawn from value-added estimates. Validity can be understood as the extent to which interpretations of scores are warranted by the evidence and theory supporting a particular use of that assessment (AERA, APA, & NCME, 1999). Validity depends in part on how educators respond to student assessments, on how well the assessments are aligned with the content in a given course, and on how well students' prior test scores account for their prior knowledge of newly tested content.

In addition, policymakers may wish to consider the extent to which student assessments are vertically scaled so that scores fall on a comparable scale from year to year. Vertically scaled tests can, in theory, be used to assess students' growth in knowledge in a given content area. In their absence, estimates of students' progress are based on their test performance relative to their peers in a given subject from year to year. However, vertical scaling is very challenging across a large number of grade levels and in cases where tested content is not closely aligned from one grade to the next (Martineau, 2006).

The report also discusses the merits and limitations of additional student performance measures that states or districts might use. Commercial interim assessments are relatively easy to administer consistently across a school system, but they are not typically designed for use in high-stakes teacher assessments, and attaching high-stakes use may undermine their utility in informing teachers' instructional decisions. Locally developed assessments have the potential to be well aligned with local curricula, but items need to be developed, administered, and scored in ways that promote high levels of consistency. Using aggregate student performance measures to evaluate teachers in nontested subjects or grades allows school systems to rely on existing measures but creates a two-tiered system in which some teachers are evaluated differently from others. In addition, policymakers must consider how teachers will be held accountable for students who receive instruction from multiple teachers in the same subject in a given year.

How New Teacher Evaluation Systems Are Addressing Measurement Challenges

To describe how educational systems are beginning to address some of the aforementioned measurement challenges, the report presents profiles of two states and three districts that have begun or are planning to incorporate measures of student performance into their teacher evaluation systems. These are Denver, Colorado; Hillsborough County, Florida; the state of Tennessee; Washington, D.C.; and the state of Delaware. To identify these five, we collected information from the websites of systems incorporating some type of student performance measures into their teacher evaluations according to media reports, prior studies, and teacher-quality websites we reviewed. The five profiles describe the student assessments administered by these systems and how those assessments are or will eventually be included in teachers' evaluations. In addition, the profiles illustrate a few steps that systems are taking to promote the reliability and validity of teachers' value-added estimates, such as averaging teachers' estimates across multiple years and administering pretests that are closely aligned with end-of-course posttests. They also demonstrate how the systems evaluate teachers in nontested subjects and grades. Finally, we use the profiles to discuss how some of the systems assign teachers responsibility for students enrolled during only a portion of the school year.

Policy Recommendations

The report offers five policy recommendations drawn from our literature review and case studies. The recommendations, which focus on approaches to consider when incorporating student achievement measures into teacher evaluation systems, are as follows:

- Create comprehensive evaluation systems that incorporate multiple measures of teacher effectiveness.
- Attend not only to the technical properties of student assessments but also to how the assessments are being used in high-stakes contexts.
- Promote consistency in the student performance measures that teachers are allowed to choose.
- Use multiple years of student achievement data in value-added estimation, and, where possible, use average teachers' value-added estimates across multiple years.
- Find ways to hold teachers accountable for students who are not included in their value-added estimates.

We conclude with the reminder that efforts to incorporate student performance into teacher evaluation systems will require experimentation, and that implementation will not always proceed as planned. In the midst of enhancing their evaluation systems, policymakers may benefit from attending to what other systems are doing and learning from their struggles and successes along the way.

Acknowledgments

The authors would like to thank the Center for American Progress for commissioning this report, and particularly Robin Chait, Raegen Miller, and Cynthia Brown for their helpful advice and feedback on the draft manuscript. Both the Center for American Progress and RAND are grateful to the Bill and Melinda Gates Foundation for generously providing support for this work. We are also grateful for research assistance provided by Xiao Wang and administrative assistance by Kate Barker, both of RAND. In addition, the report benefitted from a RAND quality assurance review by Cathleen Stasz; from technical peer reviews by Amy Holcombe, Executive Director of Talent Development for Guilford County Schools, and Jane Hannaway, Director of the Education Policy Center at the Urban Institute; and from editing by Erin-Elizabeth Johnson at RAND. Finally, we appreciate the individuals who responded to our inquiries about the profiled school systems, including Hella Bel Hadj Amor and Simon Rodberg in the Washington, D.C., Public Schools; Ina Helmick in the Hillsborough County Public Schools; Chris Wright in the Denver Public Schools; and Wayne Barton in the Delaware Department of Education.

Abbreviations

AP	Advanced Placement
CSAP	Colorado Student Assessment Program
DIBELS	Dynamic Indicators of Basic Early Literacy Skills
DPAS	Delaware Performance Appraisal System
ECE	end-of-course examination
FCAT	Florida Comprehensive Assessment Test
MAP	Merit Award Program
STAR	Special Teachers Are Rewarded
TIF	Teacher Incentive Fund
TCAP	Tennessee Comprehensive Assessment Program
TVAAS	Tennessee Value-Added Assessment System

CHAPTER ONE

Introduction

The Problem: Teachers' Evaluations Do Not Typically Reflect Their Effectiveness in Improving Student Performance

Research during the past 15 years has provided overwhelming evidence corroborating what parents and students have long suspected: that teachers vary markedly in their effectiveness in helping students learn. This body of research, conducted mainly by economists and statisticians, has capitalized on the increasing availability of databases that link students' annual standardized test scores from state accountability systems to the students' individual teachers. This work has used a class of statistical techniques called *value-added models*, which attempt to control for a variety of student, school, and classroom characteristics, including students' prior achievement, in order to isolate the average effect of a given teacher on his or her students' learning. Though the models include a variety of specifications that are being refined regularly, they have yielded several important insights that may have helped shaped policymakers' efforts to improve public education:

- Teachers are the most important school-based determinant of student learning as measured by standardized tests (Rivkin et al., 2005; Sanders & Horn, 1998; Sanders & Rivers, 1996).
- Differences in teacher effectiveness have important consequences for students: A one-standard-deviation difference in teacher effectiveness is associated with a difference of at least 10 percent of a standard deviation in students' tested achievement (Aaronson et al., 2007; Rivkin et al., 2005; Rockoff, 2004)—equivalent to moving a student from about the 50th to the 54th percentile in one year.[1] Moreover, repeated assignment to a stronger teacher seems to have a cumulative positive effect (Sanders & Rivers, 1996).
- The way in which teachers are currently rewarded in the labor market bears very little relation to their effectiveness in raising students' tested achievement (Vigdor, 2008).

A key reason for the latter state of affairs is that traditional teacher salary schedules are based on a teacher's education level and years of experience. Unfortunately, however, teaching experience bears only a small relationship to teachers' effectiveness in raising student achievement, and the relationship exists only in the first few years of a teacher's career (Aaronson et al., 2007; Clotfelter et al., 2007a, 2007b; Goldhaber, 2006; Harris & Sass, 2008; Rivkin et al., 2005; Rockoff, 2004). Though some evidence suggests that teachers with stronger academic backgrounds produce larger achievement gains than their counterparts (Ferguson & Ladd,

---

[1] Assumes that students' test scores are normally distributed.

1996; Goldhaber, 2006; Summers & Wolfe, 1977), particularly in mathematics (Harris & Sass, 2008; Hill et al., 2005), possession of an advanced degree is largely unrelated to a teacher's ability to raise students' tested achievement (Aaronson et al., 2007; Clotfelter et al., 2007a, 2007b; Goldhaber, 2006; Harris & Sass, 2008; Rivkin et al., 2005; Rockoff, 2004). Similarly, teachers' on-the-job evaluations, which are based largely on administrators' occasional observations of teachers' classrooms, have failed to reflect the variation in teachers' ability to raise student achievement (Toch & Rothman, 2008). For example, in a recent study of 12 school districts in four states, Weisberg and colleagues (2009) found that among the many districts that use evaluation systems in which teachers are rated as either satisfactory or unsatisfactory, more than 99 percent of teachers received the satisfactory rating. Even in those districts that allowed more than two rating categories, fewer than 1 percent of teachers were rated unsatisfactory, and 94 percent received one of the top two available ratings. Nor are such findings limited to these 12 districts. In a survey of a random sample of school principals in Virginia, principals reported rating only about 1.5 percent of their teachers as incompetent in a given year, despite believing about 5 percent to be ineffective (Tucker, 1997).

In most U.S. public school systems, neither salaries nor evaluation ratings are designed to reflect the variation that exists in teachers' effectiveness. As a result, most school systems fail to remediate or weed out weak teachers, and most fail to recognize and reward superior teaching performance. Thus, such systems provide little extrinsic reward (including public recognition) for excellence on the job.

A Growing Movement to Use Student Learning to Evaluate Teachers

In recent years, researchers and policymakers have questioned the notion that students will receive a good education regardless of which teacher they are assigned (Chait & Miller, 2010; Gordon et al., 2006; Hershberg, 2005). Their skepticism arises in large part from the aforementioned value-added research, which demonstrates wide variation in teachers' impact on students' tested achievement. The increasing availability of administrative datasets that capture individual students' achievement from year to year and link these students to their teachers has led to a large uptick in the number of such value-added analyses. These datasets have become increasingly prevalent in the wake of the No Child Left Behind Act of 2001, which mandates annual testing in math and reading in grades 3–8 and once in high school, as well as testing of science in some grades.

In light of improved data quality, some researchers and policymakers have argued that school systems should be able to estimate teachers' ability to raise student achievement and use these estimates to distinguish between more- and less-effective teachers. Their argument is that using these data in personnel decisions about hiring, professional development, tenure, compensation, and termination may ultimately increase the average effectiveness of the teaching workforce (Chait & Miller, 2010; Gordon et al., 2006; Odden & Kelley, 2002). This perspective, combined with wider data availability, has led to growth in the number of states and school districts that incorporate measures of student achievement into their systems for evaluating and rewarding teachers. As of 2008, for example, 26 states plus the District of Columbia were home to at least one initiative that tied teachers' compensation levels to their classroom performance (National Center on Performance Incentives, 2008).[2]

There has also been an increase in both federal and philanthropic funding to support these efforts. In 2006 and 2007, the Bush administration awarded 34 Teacher Incentive Fund (TIF) grants to states, districts, and other public educational entities that link teachers' compensation to evaluations of their ability to raise student performance (U.S. Department of Education, 2010). Under the Obama administration, the TIF grant program was expanded from $99 million to $437 million in congressional appropriations, and 62 grants were awarded in September 2010. Using student achievement growth to reward effective teachers and principals was also a cornerstone of the Obama administration's Race to the Top grant competition, which awarded grants to 11 states and the District of Columbia in the summer of 2010. In fact, a number of states quickly revised their laws to allow the use of test scores in teacher performance evaluations in an attempt to compete successfully for the nearly $4 billion in Race to the Top funding (Associated Press, 2010).

Philanthropists, too, have contributed to the move toward evaluating teachers for their performance. For example, the Bill and Melinda Gates Foundation is currently supporting the Measures of Effective Teaching project, a large-scale effort to develop high-quality teacher evaluation instruments that are correlated with teachers' impact on student achievement (Bill and Melinda Gates Foundation, 2010b). The foundation's Empowering Effective Teachers Initiative has also funded four urban school systems—Hillsborough County, Florida; Memphis, Tennessee; Pittsburgh, Pennsylvania; and a consortium of five Los Angeles, California, charter school management organizations—to overhaul their systems for recruiting, rewarding, and retaining teachers, based in part on their effectiveness in improving student achievement (Bill and Melinda Gates Foundation, 2010a).

Purpose, Organization, and Scope of This Report

Systems that are now attempting to incorporate student achievement gains into teacher evaluations face at least two important challenges: generating valid estimates of teachers' contributions to student learning and including teachers who do not teach subjects or grades that are tested annually. This report considers these two challenges in terms of the kinds of student performance measures that educational systems might use to gauge teachers' effectiveness in a variety of grades and subject areas. We begin by discussing important measurement considerations that policymakers should be aware of when using student achievement data to inform teacher evaluations, including issues of reliability, validity, and scaling. We also discuss the merits and limitations of additional student performance measures that states or districts might use, and we describe challenges that arise in deciding which students teachers should be held accountable for. We then present profiles of five state or district educational systems that have begun or are planning to incorporate measures of student performance into their teacher evaluation systems, and we synthesize lessons from the five profiles about how the systems are addressing some of the challenges they face. Finally, we offer recommendations for

---

[2] Some of these initiatives were locally based and small in scope, and only a subset of them incorporated value-added measures of student learning (National Center on Performance Incentives, 2008).

policymakers about factors to consider when incorporating student achievement measures into teacher evaluation systems.

This report focuses primarily on the use of student performance measures to evaluate teachers' effectiveness rather than specifically on the consequences attached to those evaluations. In two of the systems we profile (Denver, Colorado, and Washington, D.C.), teachers' evaluations have consequences for compensation as well as other types of personnel decisions, such as the identification, remediation, and possible termination of ineffective teachers. The other systems we profile are still in various stages of development but may eventually choose to link any number of rewards and consequences to teachers' evaluations.

CHAPTER TWO
Using Multiple Measures to Assess Teachers' Effectiveness

The new generation of performance-based evaluation systems incorporates more than one type of measure of teacher effectiveness for two reasons. The first reason is that multiple measures provide a more complete and stable picture of teaching performance than can be obtained from measures based solely on scores on standardized tests. Even with the advances in value-added modeling, in practice, most value-added systems have a number of limitations: The tests on which they are based tend to be incomplete measures of the constructs of interest, year-to-year scaling is often inadequate, and student-teacher links are generally incomplete—particularly for highly mobile students or in cases of team teaching (Baker et al., 2010; Corcoran, 2010; McCaffrey et al., 2003).

One particular concern with the quality of value-added estimates is measurement error, which can result in considerable imprecision in estimating teachers' effectiveness. This is particularly problematic for teachers with relatively small classes or who teach many students whose prior student achievement records are missing, such as students who move frequently between school systems (Baker et al., 2010; Corcoran, 2010). In addition, though value-added models do attempt to control for the nonrandom assignment of students to teachers, there is some evidence that this nonrandom assignment may vary as a function of students' most recent performance. Therefore, students may be assigned to teachers in nonrandom ways that make it easier for some teachers than others to raise their students' test performance (Rothstein, 2010).

By reducing reliance on any single measure of a teacher's performance, multiple-measure systems improve the accuracy and stability of teachers' evaluations while also reducing the likelihood that teachers will engage in excessive test preparation or other forms of test-focused instruction (Booher-Jennings, 2005; Hamilton et al., 2007; Stecher et al., 2008). To this end, many new systems try to create more-valid indicators of teacher effectiveness by combining measures of student achievement growth on state tests with measures of teachers' instructional behavior (such as those based on observations by principals or lead teachers) or with diverse measures of student outcomes (such as scores on district-administered assessments).

Second, the use of multiple measures addresses a pragmatic concern: Value-added estimates can be calculated only for teachers of subjects and grades that are tested at least annually, such as those administered under a state's accountability system. In most states, the tested grades and subjects are only those required by No Child Left Behind: math and reading in grades 3–8. Testing in these grades allows for value-added estimation in grades 4–8 only because the first available score is used as a control for students' prior learning. One study in Florida reported that fewer than 31 percent of teachers in the state teach these tested subjects and grades (Prince et al., 2009). Thus, a critical policy question is how to develop evaluation systems that incorporate measures of student learning for the other teachers in the system as well.

Technical Considerations in Selecting Quality Measures of Student Performance

As states and districts seek multiple measures of student performance to incorporate into their evaluation systems, they must find student performance measures that can support inferences about teacher effectiveness in a variety of grades and content areas. When using student achievement measures to evaluate teachers' performance, the technical quality of the achievement measures is an important consideration. There are two principal aspects of technical quality with which policymakers should be concerned. The first is *reliability*, or the extent to which scores are consistent over repeated measurements and are free of errors of measurement (AERA, APA, & NCME, 1999). The second aspect is *validity*, which refers to "the degree to which accumulated evidence and theory support specific interpretations of test scores entailed by proposed uses of a test" (AERA, APA, & NCME, 1999, p. 184). Validity applies to the inference drawn from assessment results rather than to the assessment itself. If one thinks of reliability broadly as the consistency or precision of a measure, then one might conceptualize validity as the accuracy of an inference drawn from a measure. In addition, validity needs to be established for a particular purpose or application of a test. Assessments that have evidence of validity for one purpose should not be used for another purpose until there is additional validity evidence related to the latter purpose (AERA, APA, & NCME, 1999; Perie et al., 2007).

Another aspect of measurement quality that policymakers may want to consider is the extent to which scores are *vertically scaled*, meaning that they are comparable from one grade to the next. We discuss each of these sets of considerations in greater detail in the sections that follow.

Reliability Considerations

One oft-reported measure of an instrument's reliability is its internal consistency reliability, which expresses the extent to which items on the test measure the same underlying construct (Crocker & Algina, 1986). A common metric used to express internal consistency is coefficient alpha. Internal consistency reliability measures are not complete measures of reliability, as test reliability also depends on such factors as the skill level of the students taking the test, the testing conditions, and the scoring procedures for open-response items, but they do provide one widely used and readily understood indication of instrument quality. In general, scores with internal consistency reliabilities above 0.9 are considered quite reliable, those with reliabilities above 0.8 are considered acceptable, and those with reliabilities above 0.7 are considered acceptable in some situations. The U.S. Department of Education's What Works Clearinghouse, which evaluates the quality of education research, sets minimum levels of internal consistency reliability for outcome measures of between 0.5 and 0.6, depending on the quality of measures in a given topic area.[1]

Measures of internal consistency reliability do not take into account interrater reliability in the scoring of any open-response items that tests may include, and they also do not measure the reliability of the value-added estimates themselves.[2] *Interrater reliability* is an important consideration in the case of items that are assessed by human scorers (such as essays or open-

---

[1] Based on a review of several What Works Clearinghouse topic area review protocols, including beginning reading, middle school math, early childhood education, emotional and behavioral disorders, and data-driven decisionmaking.

[2] This topic is addressed in greater detail in a recent Center for American Progress report by Goldhaber (2010).

response test questions) because one wants to minimize the extent to which an individual's score on the assessment is dependent on the idiosyncrasies of the rater who happens to score it. If school systems are administering the rating of open-ended assessments, it is important that they rigorously train teachers on rubric-based scoring procedures and that they assess inter-rater reliability by examining the correlations among raters—especially chance-adjusted correlations, like Cohen's kappa—on "anchor" papers graded by multiple raters. Another way to help enhance interrater reliability is to average the ratings of two scorers on every assessment and to have a tiebreaking scorer rate papers whose two scorers' ratings are markedly different.

Reliability of value-added estimates is an important consideration because, due to random classroom- and student-level error, value-added estimates are known to be unstable from year to year. While some of that instability appears to reflect actual changes in effectiveness, studies indicate that a nontrivial portion is also due to measurement error (Goldhaber & Hansen, 2008; Lankford et al., 2010; McCaffrey et al., 2009). These studies establish that the reliability of value-added estimates improves when teachers' estimates are averaged across multiple years.[3] Though such averaging ignores any true changes in a teacher's effectiveness from year to year, educational systems may still be well advised to take this approach in order to increase the robustness of the estimates. In addition, increasing the number of years of student achievement data included in the model improves the precision of a teacher's value-added estimates, in this case by more thoroughly controlling for students' prior learning (Ballou et al., 2004; Corcoran, 2010; McCaffrey et al., 2009).

Validity Considerations

In the case of students' academic growth from year to year in a given content area, a crucial validity question is to what extent changes in a student's performance reflect actual changes in his or her understanding of the underlying content. Similarly, when student test scores are used to estimate teaching effectiveness, a validity investigation should be carried out to help users understand the extent to which those estimates accurately represent each teacher's contribution to student learning.

One important component of any validity investigation is the collection of evidence regarding various threats to the validity of inferences for a particular use of a measure. For instance, changes in student performance that resulted from better test-taking skills or from familiarity with tested questions would undermine the validity of an inference about students' content learning. Such threats can result from teachers' instructional focus on test-preparation strategies in lieu of better teaching of the underlying content (see, for example, Koretz, 2008; Koretz & Barron, 1998). Instructional practices that lead to artificially inflated scores include not only explicit test preparation but also more-subtle shifts from untested content or skills to tested content or skills, or from excessive emphasis on presenting material in a format that is similar to the format used on the test (Koretz & Hamilton, 2006).[4]

Another threat to the validity of an inference about students' academic growth could result from inconsistencies in the content tested from one year to the next (McCaffrey et al., 2003). For example, if a student's growth in science knowledge is estimated using differences in his or her performance on a recent chemistry test and a prior biology test, at least a por-

---

[3]   See also Schochet and Chiang (2010).

[4]   For a framework describing a range of instructional responses to high-stakes tests, see Koretz and Hamilton (2006).

tion of that difference might be attributable to the student's prior chemistry knowledge that was not captured by the biology test rather than to any actual change in the student's scientific knowledge that occurred between the two test administrations. Even efforts to measure growth in such subjects as reading and mathematics can be hindered by shifts in the coverage of specific topics or skills from one grade to the next (Martineau, 2006; Schmidt et al., 2005). For example, if a grade 4 math test focuses primarily on arithmetic skills and the grade 5 test focuses mainly on fractions and decimals, then students' performance on the grade 4 test will not fully capture their prior knowledge of material tested in grade 5.

A related problem involves attributing student performance to individual teachers when the assessments are intended to cover material from multiple courses. For instance, high school exit examinations and college entrance examinations, such as the SAT or ACT, include content that students are expected to have learned throughout high school. Attributing students' performance in a given subject on these tests to a particular teacher would be difficult because the student would generally have no prior assessments on record of similarly weighted content in each of the prior high school years.

Vertical Scaling

A vertically scaled test is one in which the performance scale is designed to be consistent from one grade to the next, so that, for example, a student's score in grade 8 math can be directly compared to his or her score in grade 7, grade 5, or even grade 3 math, showing the amount of progress made in the interim. While vertical scaling is always difficult when content demands change from grade to grade, the advantage of vertical scaling in a value-added system is that value-added estimates should—at least theoretically—reflect students' true growth in understanding from year to year. In contrast, when using tests that are not vertically scaled, it is generally students' relative standing in comparison with their peers that is being compared from one grade to the next. Insofar as content in one grade builds directly on content from prior grades, vertically scaled assessments therefore allow comparisons of students' absolute learning rather than relative standing in a given content area (McCaffrey et al., 2003). In subjects and grades in which content is closely aligned from one grade to the next, as may be the case in reading and elementary mathematics, vertical scaling can provide a considerable advantage in measuring students' learning progress. It is nevertheless important to remember that, when there is limited overlap of content tested from one grade to the next (e.g., a focus on arithmetic one year and fractions and decimals the next), vertical scaling becomes especially challenging, and the broader the grade span, the greater the difficulty. Thus, there are distinct and important limitations to the absolute amount of learning growth that vertically scaled tests can identify (Martineau, 2006).

Measuring Student Performance in Grades and Subjects That Are Not Assessed Annually

States and districts that wish to incorporate measures of student performance into teacher evaluation systems need to find ways of measuring student performance in subjects and grades that are not tested by annual state accountability tests. One way to approach this task is to purchase commercial assessments for use in nontested grades and subjects. These may take the form of summative assessments, much like the state accountability tests, that measure students' learning over the duration of an entire course. They may also include interim or benchmark assessments that are designed to be administered as diagnostic tools throughout the year. An alternative approach would be for a system to develop its own summative or interim assessments.

The advantage of buying commercial tests is that they will likely have already been designed to meet standards of internal consistency reliability and demonstrate predictive validity with other measures of similar content. They may also offer useful score-reporting tools to help educators interpret and understand their students' performance. However, even most commercial tests typically have not been validated for use in evaluations of teachers' effectiveness. Also, it is important for systems using commercial measures to ensure that the content they test is consistent with the content teachers are being asked to teach in each grade and subject level. Otherwise, the tests will not provide useful measures of teachers' effectiveness. Moreover, if tests are designed as interim assessments, they will likely have been developed to inform rather than evaluate teachers' classroom decisions. This is an important consideration, because tests developed or validated for one purpose should not be used for other purposes without evidence that their scores yield valid, reliable inferences in the "off-label" contexts (AERA, APA, & NCME, 1999). For example, attaching high stakes to tests that are designed to inform teachers' instructional decisions may dilute the tests' diagnostic value, especially if teachers attempt to boost students' scores on the interim tests rather than using the tests to identify strengths and weaknesses in students' understanding.

Educational systems that develop their own assessments have the advantage of being able to include content that is well aligned with state standards and local curricula, but they may not have the resources or expertise to carefully assess the reliability of their measures or to gauge their validity in high-stakes contexts. Sometimes, measures developed in-house include assessments of students' task performance, such as grade-level writing prompts or portfolio assessments of student work. Such measures may be valued for testing skills not easily measured by multiple-choice tests (LeMahieu et al., 1995), but performance tasks are subject to at least two important limitations that policymakers should be aware of. First, due to the risk of score corruption, teachers should not assess their own students (Koretz, 2008). Second, scorers should be trained and periodically tested to ensure a reasonable level of interrater reliability. In addition, the conditions under which the writing prompts or portfolio assessments are administered must be rigorously standardized to ensure that differences in student performance are not attributable to differences in the level of assessment guidance and support provided in each classroom. Classroom-level differences in guidance are of particular concern in portfolio and other performance assessments, where teachers may vary considerably in the amount of structure and explicit guidance they offer to students. A RAND study of portfolio assessments in Vermont, for example, found that students' portfolio scores lacked sufficient reliability for high-stakes use due both to variation in the complexity of sampled tasks and to weak rates of interrater agreement (Klein et al., 1995).

Still other systems may choose to use aggregate (e.g., schoolwide or departmentwide) student performance growth to assess teachers in nontested grades and subjects. One advantage of basing teachers' evaluations on aggregate school performance measures is that it may encourage teachers to collaborate with peers and align their curriculum with teachers in other grades. An obvious disadvantage, however, is that it can create a two-tiered system in which some teachers are held accountable for the performance gains of their own students and other teachers are held accountable for the performance of a broader set of students than those they currently teach.

Assigning Teachers Responsibility for Students' Performance

As educational systems begin attaching high stakes to student performance measures, they also face a number of important decisions about which students' performance teachers will be held responsible for. These challenges can be particularly complicated in cases where more than one teacher delivers instruction to a student in a given subject and year. This occurs, for instance, when students enroll in a teacher's class for only part of the year, receive supplemental instruction from a special education teacher or after-school instructor, or enroll in a class where multiple teachers work as a team to teach the same content area.

In the case of students who change teachers (or even schools) during the year, a key question is what proportion of the student's performance should be attributed to the teacher who is teaching that student at the time of testing. Research currently in progress at RAND suggests that this issue is less straightforward than it seems because the performance of students for whom teachers have only a small fraction of responsibility can have a disproportionate impact on the teacher's value-added estimate. Until studies that provide more-definitive guidance become available, systems might be advised to assign teachers responsibility only for students who spend most of the year with them. For instance, the Gates Foundation's Measures of Effective Teaching study, which RAND is helping to conduct, holds teachers accountable only for students who are enrolled in their classes for at least 90 percent of the school year.

The cases of supplemental instruction and team teaching may be even more challenging, since it is nearly impossible to determine which teacher may be driving students' performance growth and whether each teacher's impact is, in fact, proportional to the time he or she spends with the students. Because making individual attributions in supplemental or team teaching environments is so difficult, one reasonable approach is simply to assign equal student performance ratings to members of a teaching team and allow other measures (such as classroom observations or contributions to the school community) to distinguish between the teamed teachers.

Another challenge in apportioning responsibility for student performance is simply obtaining high-quality data that accurately reflect the proportion of instructional time a student spent with each teacher in a given subject. One way to promote data accuracy is to give teachers an opportunity to periodically review their rosters in the data system and confirm the proportion of time each student was enrolled in their class and taught by them (rather than by a supplemental teacher). One school system that uses this approach is the Houston Independent School District, which maintains a student verification system that teachers can log into in order to confirm the accuracy of their rosters (Houston Independent School District, 2010).

Finally, it seems prudent to exclude from teachers' value-added calculations those students who do not have prior test scores on file in the district because, without such scores, it is impossible to hold constant those students' prior achievement in a given subject. A possible downside of excluding students from teachers' value-added calculations—including not only students without prior tests scores but also those who have changed teachers during the year, etc.—is that teachers may then have a weaker incentive to focus on these students' learning (Corcoran, 2010). A possible policy solution is to develop supplemental ways of holding teachers accountable for these students, such as requiring them to set individual performance goals on teacher-chosen measures for those students.

CHAPTER THREE

How Are New Teacher Evaluation Systems Incorporating Multiple Measures?

We selected five systems to examine how new teacher evaluation systems are incorporating measures of student performance beyond the tested grades and subjects required by No Child Left Behind. To identify these five, we first collected information from the websites of systems incorporating some type of student performance measures into their teacher evaluations according to reports by the National Center on Performance Incentives (2008) and the National Comprehensive Center for Teacher Quality (2010).[1] We also examined the websites of evaluation systems we were aware of from media reports or prior RAND research.

The five selected systems represent some of the most well-documented models for incorporating measures of student performance into teacher evaluations. Two programs—the Tennessee Teacher Evaluation System and the Delaware Performance Appraisal System II—are state-level systems, and the other three—based in Denver, Colorado; Hillsborough County, Florida; and Washington, D.C.—are district-level systems. These programs are particularly interesting because of the distinctive ways they have found or are seeking to incorporate student performance into their teacher evaluation systems. We also note that these systems are still evolving and that, as they are implemented, they will continue to be shaped and refined along the way.

In the sections that follow, we describe each of the five systems along several dimensions: year of initial implementation, subjects and grades tested by state or other accountability tests, and evaluation component categories for teachers in tested and nontested subjects and grades. Data about the evaluation systems were collected primarily from the public websites. When possible, we also conducted conversations or email exchanges with staff members in the systems. The particular details we present are accurate as of the date of this report, but it is likely that system elements will be modified as sites learn from the experience of managing these systems and refine their approaches.

---

[1] Evaluation systems we investigated beyond those highlighted in this report include Harrison County, Colorado's District 2; Cincinnati's Teacher Evaluation System; Houston's Accelerating Student Progress, Increasing Results and Expectations system; Memphis's Teacher Effectiveness Initiative; Minnesota's Q-Comp program; Pittsburgh's Research-Based Inclusive System of Evaluation; a newly approved teacher evaluation system in Seattle; and newly authorized statewide teacher evaluation plans in Colorado and New York. We chose the five systems described here primarily because they have already made progress toward incorporating student performance into teachers' evaluations and because they have made public a considerable amount of documentation about their respective approaches.

Denver ProComp

First implemented in the 2005–2006 academic year, Denver's ProComp teacher evaluation and compensation system is the oldest of the teacher evaluation systems profiled in this report (Mitchell, 2005).[2] The program, which is voluntary for teachers hired before January 1, 2006, and mandatory for those hired thereafter, offers evaluations and evaluation-linked incentives in four categories: knowledge and skills (including completion of professional development units), comprehensive professional evaluation (based on principal observations), market incentives (for teaching in hard-to-staff schools and subject areas), and student growth (including value-added and other approaches described later in this section) (Denver Public Schools, 2010c). As of May 2007, nearly half of the teachers in the district were being evaluated under the ProComp system (DeGrow, 2007). Table 3.1 describes the program's key components.

It is important to understand that ProComp is a comprehensive teacher evaluation and reward plan that evaluates teachers according to the aforementioned dimensions and rewards them accordingly. The first three categories of evaluations and incentives apply identically to all teachers enrolled in ProComp, though the second category, comprehensive professional evaluation, is the only component that also applies to teachers who are not enrolled in ProComp. Probationary teachers are evaluated at least two times a year, and nonprobationary teachers are evaluated informally every year and formally at least once every three years (Denver Public Schools, 2008). The comprehensive professional evaluation rates teachers as exceeding, meeting, developing, or not meeting expectations in five categories of performance based on principals' observations of their instruction. Teachers who are rated as exceeding, meeting, or developing in all five categories are then rated as satisfactory; others are rated as unsatisfactory and referred for remediation. A satisfactory rating also earns a bonus of between $376 and $1,127 for teachers enrolled in ProComp.

For ProComp teachers, the student growth component is a complement to the comprehensive professional evaluation and other program dimensions. It includes three subcom-

Table 3.1
Key Components of Denver ProComp

Key Component	Description
First implementation year	2005–2006
Subjects and grades tested by the state accountability test	Math, reading, and writing in grades 3–10 Science in grades 5, 8, and 10
Subjects and grades tested by other standardized tests	Not applicable
Evaluation components for teachers in tested subjects or grades	Knowledge and skills Comprehensive professional evaluation Market incentives Student growth[a]
Evaluation components for teachers in nontested subjects or grades	Same as for teachers in tested subjects and grades, except the individual teacher value-added component is excluded

[a] This category includes teacher-selected assessments, schoolwide student performance, and individual value added.

---

[2] However, some programs described here are based on the older value-added or pay-for-performance systems on which the new evaluation systems are built.

ponents based on (1) teacher-selected assessments, (2) schoolwide student performance, and (3) individual teacher value added (Denver Public Schools, 2010a). Specifically, under subcomponent 1, teachers of any subject and grade can set two student growth goals using measures of the teacher's choice that are approved by a supervisor. Such measures might include a benchmark test, curriculum test, or teacher-developed assessment but cannot include the state accountability test, which is part of subcomponents 2 and 3. Published examples for career and technical education suggest that student growth goals should specify a performance objective (e.g., the percentage of students expected to reach a specified performance or improvement target), the rationale for the objective, the population to whom the objective applies (e.g., students with at least an 85-percent attendance rate), the assessments to be used (e.g., pretests, posttests, rubrics), the expected amount of performance gain or growth, the content to be learned, and the teacher's strategy for helping students achieve the goal (Denver Public Schools, 2006). Teachers who meet at least one of the two goals they set under this subcomponent receive a 1-percent salary bonus based on an index salary of $37,551. If both goals are met, this bonus is added to their salary base.

Under subcomponent 2, ProComp teachers can be rewarded for reaching the school-level performance goals, which include 6.4-percent non–base-building bonuses (again, based on the index salary) for working in a school with especially high student performance or strong growth on the state accountability test, the Colorado Student Assessment Program (CSAP). Subcomponent 3, the final student growth category, which uses individual teacher value-added estimates, is awarded to teachers whose students exceed expected average growth on the CSAP. Because students are tested annually only in math, reading, and writing in grades 3–10, only teachers of these subjects in grades 4–10 are eligible to be evaluated and receive the non–base-building 6.4-percent bonus in this category (Denver Public Schools, 2010b).

Hillsborough County's Empowering Effective Teachers Initiative

In the 2010–2011 academic year, Hillsborough County, Florida, is planning its 2011–2012 implementation of the Empowering Effective Teachers Initiative. Through this initiative, sponsored by the Gates Foundation, the district aims to include student performance in evaluations of all its teachers. The Hillsborough County Public School District has been participating in state-level teacher pay-for-performance initiatives since 2006, so its new evaluation program will build on that infrastructure. The first of these initiatives was Florida's Special Teachers Are Rewarded (STAR) plan, which was followed in 2007 by an amended and more flexible policy called the Merit Award Program (MAP) (Buddin et al., 2007; Center for Educator Compensation Reform, 2007). Both of these programs offered bonuses for teachers who were evaluated positively by principals and who raised students to higher levels of proficiency on the Florida Comprehensive Assessment Test (FCAT), which tests students annually in mathematics, reading, science, and writing in grades 3–11. Table 3.2 describes the program's key components.

Under STAR, principal evaluations and students' standardized test performance each received equal weighting in teachers' performance evaluations; under MAP, student performance is weighted at 60 percent. The new Empowering Effective Teachers program, in contrast, will base 60 percent of each teacher's evaluation rating on classroom observations. Half of this classroom observation rating will be based on the principal's observations and the other

Table 3.2
Key Components of Hillsborough County's Empowering Effective Teachers Initiative

Key Component	Description
First implementation year	Planned for 2011–2012, but builds on state systems that began in 2005–2006
Subjects and grades tested by the state accountability test	Math, reading, science, and writing in grades 3–11
Subjects and grades tested by other standardized tests	556 end-of-course examinations available New test development also planned
Evaluation components for teachers in tested subjects or grades	60% classroom observations (30% by the principal, 30% by a mentor/peer advisor) 40% student learning gains (namely, individual value added)
Evaluation components for teachers in nontested subjects or grades	Same as for teachers in tested subjects and grades because the objective is that value-added estimates will be available for all teachers

half on observations by a trained mentor or peer evaluator. The other 40 percent will be based on student learning gains as measured by student achievement growth on standardized tests.

To implement this plan, Hillsborough County will draw on a large set of end-of-course examinations (ECEs) it has constructed over the past two decades to meet the longstanding requirement that such tests be administered in all subjects and grades taught in the district. These end-of-course examinations, many of which are accompanied by pretests, exist for a broad array of subjects not tested by state examinations, including foreign languages, art, music, career/technical education, and even physical education. As of May 2007, more than 500 exams linked to 429 different course numbers had been created (School District of Hillsborough County, 2007). Between 2007 and 2009, the exams were made available statewide as part of Florida's End-of-Course Examination Clearinghouse. The clearinghouse is no longer funded, but Hillsborough County teachers continue to administer the pretests and posttests linked to their individual courses.[3] However, for reasons of test security, the exams are not publicly available, so it is difficult to gauge the range of questions and tasks they entail.

A limitation of the end-of-course examinations in Hillsborough County is that the locally developed tests may not have been subject to rigorous validation and testing, and there is no technical documentation available for the tests. When the tests were available statewide, some school districts that attempted to use them reported finding errors in some tests (Center for Educator Compensation Reform, 2007), though the clearinghouse's website cautioned districts to review the tests before using them (School District of Hillsborough County, 2007).

Hillsborough County reports that it plans to construct new, improved pretests and posttests during the 2011–2012 academic year (Hillsborough County Public Schools, 2010). Moreover, the state of Florida is developing end-of-course exams on which Hillsborough County may be able to draw. The first such exam, for Algebra I, will be administered in May 2011 (Florida Department of Education, 2010).

---

[3] Personal communication with Ina Helmick of the Hillsborough County Schools' Department of Assessment and Accountability, October 30, 2010.

The Tennessee Teacher Evaluation System

In an effort to be more competitive in the first round of the federal Race to the Top competition (which it won, along with Delaware), Tennessee passed a new Teacher Evaluation System into law in January 2010 (Associated Press, 2010; Locker, 2010). The new system, which will take effect in the 2011–2012 academic year, builds on a longstanding program in the state called the Tennessee Value-Added Assessment System (TVAAS). Developed in Tennessee by statistician William Sanders in 1992, the TVAAS has long provided value-added estimates of teacher effectiveness that were supplied confidentially to teachers and school principals each year. Prior to passage of the new Teacher Evaluation System in 2010, these estimates could be referenced in teachers' evaluations but could not provide a formal basis for the evaluation rating (DeLacy, 1999–2009; Locker, 2010), which was instead based on two to three classroom observations per year (Tennessee Department of Education, n.d.-b). Table 3.3 describes the program's key components.

In contrast, under the new Teacher Evaluation System set to take effect in 2011, 35 percent of a teacher's evaluation will be based on the teacher's value-added estimates in subjects and grades tested by the Tennessee Comprehensive Assessment Program (TCAP), the state accountability testing system used in Tennessee (Locker, 2010). As of the 2009–2010 academic year, tested subjects and grades included grades 3–8 in math, reading/language arts, science, and social studies (with district-optional tests available in grades K–2), as well as end-of-course tests in Algebra I, Biology I, English I and II, and U.S. History (Tennessee Department of Education, 2010a, 2010b). Additional tests are still planned for development, including end-of-course tests in Geometry, Algebra II, Chemistry, Physics, and English III. The value-added component for teachers of difficult-to-test subjects, such as art and music, may be based on schoolwide academic growth if a recent recommendation by members of the Teacher Evaluation Advisory Committee is implemented (Zelinski, 2010).

Under the new legislation, an additional 15 percent of a teacher's evaluation will be based on other measures of student achievement that are "yet to be developed—such as reading assessments for elementary teachers and college entrance tests, end-of-year subject tests and advance-placement tests for high school teachers" (Locker, 2010). The other 50 percent of a

Table 3.3
Key Components of the Tennessee Teacher Evaluation System

Key Component	Description
First implementation year	Planned for 2011–2012, but builds on a statewide value-added system dating back to 1992
Subjects and grades tested by the state accountability test	Math, reading, science, and social studies in grades 3–8 (with math, reading, and science testing being optional in grades K–2)
Subjects and grades tested by other standardized tests	End-of-course exams given in Algebra I, Biology I, English I and II, and U.S. History Additional tests planned for Geometry, Algebra II, Chemistry, Physics, and English III
Evaluation components for teachers in tested subjects or grades	50% principal observations 35% individual value-added estimates from state standardized tests and end-of course assessments 15% student performance on other tests yet to be developed
Evaluation components for teachers in nontested subjects or grades	The value-added component for teachers of nontested subjects may be based on schoolwide academic growth, but this is still being decided

teacher's evaluation will be based on principal observations similar to those already conducted as part of the teacher's evaluation process; these may be supplemented with personal conferences and evaluation surveys from supervisors, peers, and students (Zelinski, 2010). If another recommendation by the Teacher Evaluation Advisory Committee is carried out, the observations may be briefer but more frequent than before, including as many as four observations per teacher per year (Zelinski, 2010).

Washington, D.C., IMPACT

In the 2009–2010 academic year, the District of Columbia Public Schools began implementing a new performance-based teacher evaluation system called IMPACT. As in Denver's program, the extent to which a teacher's evaluation is based on value-added measures of student learning depends on whether he or she teaches tested subjects and grades.[4] Because the D.C. Comprehensive Assessment System currently tests students only in math and reading in grades 3–8, value-added estimates are available only for teachers of these subjects in grades 4–8. For these teachers, 50 percent of the evaluation score is based on the teacher's individual value-added contribution to student achievement gains. Thirty-five percent of the score is based on five classroom observations per year using a district-developed rubric; three observations are conducted by a school administrator and two by an impartial "master educator" who is not located at the school site (District of Columbia Public Schools, 2009b, p. 14). Ten percent of the evaluation score is based on demonstrated commitment to the school community, including outreach to parents and collaboration with colleagues, and 5 percent is based on school-wide student achievement growth. Table 3.4 describes the program's key components.

Table 3.4
Key Components of the D.C. IMPACT Program

Key Component	Description
First implementation year	2009–2010
Subjects and grades tested by the state accountability test	Math and reading in grades 3–8 Science in grades 5 and 8 Biology I
Subjects and grades tested by other standardized tests	Additional test development is planned
Evaluation components for teachers in tested subjects or grades	35% administrator or master educator observations 50% individual value added 10% commitment to the school community 5% schoolwide value added Attendance and punctuality also considered
Evaluation components for teachers in nontested subjects or grades	75% administrator or master educator observation 10% student growth on a teacher-chosen measure 10% commitment to the school community 5% schoolwide value added Attendance and punctuality also considered

---

[4] Though IMPACT did not initially include a differentiated compensation component, teacher contract negotiations concluded in April 2010 resulted in the supplemental creation of IMPACT*plus*, which will eventually include a pay-for-performance component for some teachers (District of Columbia Public Schools, 2010a).

The stated long-term plan for the IMPACT program is to develop additional tests so that more teachers have individual value-added estimates available. Meanwhile, 10 percent of the evaluation score for general education teachers of nontested grades and subjects is still based on contributions to the school community, and 5 percent is still based on schoolwide achievement growth. However, in the absence of value-added scores, 75 percent of the evaluation score is based on administrator and master educator observations, and 10 percent is based on students' demonstrated growth on "teacher-assessed student achievement data" (District of Columbia Public Schools, 2009c, p. 36).

Teacher-assessed student achievement data can include a variety of standards-aligned assessments chosen by the teacher and approved by a school administrator. The district specifies a set of growth and mastery targets that students must meet and sets the weights assigned to each target, but teachers can choose the standards-aligned assessments they use to measure each target. For most content areas, they can select "off-the-shelf" (i.e., commercial) or "teacher-created" assessments (District of Columbia Public Schools, 2010b). To demonstrate growth, teachers must administer both a pretest and posttest. The district also specifies the student performance levels associated with each teacher rating level. For instance, in secondary social studies, a class average of 90 percent on a standards-aligned, teacher-created or off-the-shelf assessment indicates a high level of teacher performance on that target. Elementary physical education teachers, on the other hand, can demonstrate high performance on the physical fitness target if students show growth, on average, in four of five measures of fitness, such as aerobic capacity, flexibility, and muscular strength (District of Columbia Public Schools, 2010b).

Special education teachers are assessed much like teachers of nontested grades, but their evaluations also have components for developing and helping students meet appropriate Individual Education Plan goals (District of Columbia Public Schools, 2009d). IMPACT also includes evaluations for noninstructional school staff (such as counselors, librarians, and office staff) that are linked to both observed job performance and schoolwide academic achievement growth (District of Columbia Public Schools, 2009a).

The Delaware Performance Appraisal System II

Delaware maintains a comprehensive teacher evaluation system called the Delaware Performance Appraisal System (DPAS) II, which was piloted in 2005 and broadly implemented in 2007. The system includes components for teachers' planning and preparation, classroom environment, instruction, professional responsibilities, and student improvement. However, rather than incorporating value-added measures of teachers' impact on achievement, the student improvement component currently focuses on teachers' ability both to use data to set goals for student performance and to measure students' progress toward those goals (Delaware Department of Education, 2008b). In particular, teachers must demonstrate that they use assessment and accountability data to establish annual student learning goals, use assessments that measure progress toward those goals, use measureable evidence to show students' progress toward those goals, and reflect upon and share progress data as appropriate. However, to comply with its Race to the Top grant implementation plan, the state is now considering various ways to estimate teachers' value added in subjects other than math, reading, and writing, which are tested each year in grades 3–10 (Delaware Department of Education, 2009).[5] Table 3.5 describes the program's key components.

Though its use of student performance to inform teacher evaluations is still entirely in the planning stages, Delaware is an interesting case because it has made public its considerations about how to refine the system to include value-added measures of teacher effectiveness (Delaware Department of Education, 2010). This information enables us to examine the measures under consideration. As other Race to the Top winners begin to revise or augment their teacher evaluation systems to include measures of student performance, they are likely to face similar dilemmas and may benefit from understanding another state's deliberations.

To provide assessments in the early grades, Delaware is reportedly considering commercial diagnostic assessments, such as the Dynamic Indicators of Basic Early Literacy Skills (DIBELS), an early reading test administered statewide, and the Gates-MacGinitie Reading Test, another commercially available diagnostic reading assessment used in some Delaware districts (Delaware Department of Education, 2010). The state has also reportedly considered using districtwide common assessments, including districtwide writing prompts and student portfolio measures. In addition, the state has considered using student performance on Advanced Placement (AP) exams as measures of teachers' effectiveness. However, they acknowledge that because students who take AP tests are typically a self-selected group, and because these examinations test advanced levels of knowledge, the difficulty of using them for teacher evaluations lies in establishing that a student's prior test scores adequately control for his or her prior knowledge in the tested domain (Delaware Department of Education, 2010).

It is also interesting to consider the measures that Delaware has reportedly decided not to use. These include college entrance examination scores, which the state considers "not valid for this purpose" (Delaware Department of Education, 2010). The state has also decided not to rely on teacher-created tests because these are not comparable across classrooms, and it

Table 3.5
Key Components of Delaware's Performance Appraisal System II

Key Component	Description
First implementation year	Piloted in 2005 and broadly implemented in 2007, but the component incorporating student performance is still in the planning stage
Subjects and grades tested by the state accountability test	Math and reading in grades 2–10 Science and social studies in grades 4, 6, 8, and 11 Writing in grades 3–11
Subjects and grades tested by other standardized tests	Additional measures are under consideration
Evaluation components for teachers in tested subjects or grades	Equal weight assigned to • planning and preparation • classroom environment • instruction • professional responsibilities • student improvement[a]
Evaluation components for teachers in nontested subjects or grades	Same, for now, as teachers in tested subjects and grades, though this could change as student performance measures are incorporated

[a] Student improvement does not yet (but will eventually) include measures of student performance.

---

[5]   Delaware tests science and social studies in grades 4, 6, 8, and 11 (Delaware Department of Education, 2009).

has chosen not to attach stakes to students' attendance. Finally, Delaware has decided not to use student discipline statistics or parent surveys as measures of student growth, though it acknowledges that these may be appropriate for other components of a teacher's evaluation (Delaware Department of Education, 2010).

CHAPTER FOUR

How Are the New Teacher Evaluation Systems Addressing Key Measurement Quality Challenges?

The five evaluation systems profiled in Chapter Three were chosen because they exhibit distinct ways of incorporating student performance measures into teachers' evaluations. In this chapter, we review and discuss what is known about how these systems are addressing some of the measurement and attribution challenges identified earlier in this report. We first describe what is known about the reliability and scaling of the assessments administered by these systems and how the systems are addressing common validity concerns. We then discuss ways in which the systems are measuring student growth for teachers of nontested grades and subjects. Finally, we discuss how the systems are seeking to address some of the challenges of assigning teachers responsibility for particular students' learning.

Reliability Considerations

We first examined what was known about the technical quality of the student performance measures already in use in the five systems described in this report, examining not only measures for reading and mathematics but also those for science, social studies, and writing, where applicable. One area in which we found considerable evidence concerned the internal consistency reliability estimates of the existing measures. These estimates, expressed in terms of either Cronbach's or stratified alphas, are summarized in Table 4.1.

What is notable from the table is that the published internal consistency reliabilities for the tests in use are quite high, ranging from about 0.84 to 0.94 across the selected states, and there is little systematic variation between states or among subject areas within states. While the internal consistency of high-stakes measures has not been a primary source of concern for many critics of value-added measures (Baker et al., 2010; Corcoran, 2010), it is noteworthy that the internal consistencies of these five states' accountability tests are quite similar.

As is evident from the table, we were not able to obtain technical reports for the TCAP. The TCAP is reported to combine items aligned with the state standards as well as items from the TerraNova (Third Edition), a nationally norm-referenced commercial test published by CTB/McGraw-Hill, so the internal consistency reliability estimates are assumed to be quite high, despite not being currently published online.

In addition, we were not able to obtain internal consistency estimates or other details of technical quality for the more than 500 end-of-course exams available in Hillsborough County. Because the tests are locally developed and may not have been technically evaluated,

Table 4.1
Test Information, Including Range of Internal Consistency Reliability Statistics for the Principal Standardized Test in Each System, Reported Across All Tested Grades, by Subject

System	Reading	Math	Science	Social Studies	Writing	Vertically Scaled?
Denver Colorado Student Assessment Program	0.88–0.94 (grades 3–10) Spanish version: 0.88–0.93 (grades 3 and 4)	0.90–0.94 (grades 3–10)	0.92–0.93 (grades 5, 8, and 10)	Not applicable	0.90–0.93 (grades 3–10) Spanish version: 0.87–0.91 (grades 3 and 4)	Yes in reading and math
Hillsborough Florida Comprehensive Assessment Test	0.852–0.896 (grades 3–10)	0.845–0.900 (grades 3–10)	Not available	Not applicable	0.847–0.857 (grades 4, 8, 10)	No
Tennessee Tennessee Comprehensive Assessment Program	Not available (however, tested in grades 3–8 and high school ECEs; grades K–2 optional)	Not available (however, tested in grades 3–8 and high school ECEs; grades K–2 optional)	Not available (however, tested in grades 3–8 and high school ECEs; grades K–2 optional)	Not available (however, tested in grades 3–8 and high school ECEs)	Not available (however, tested in grades 5, 8, 11)	Yes in grades 3–8
Washington, D.C. District of Columbia Comprehensive Assessment System[a]	0.904–0.923 (grades 3–8)	0.910–0.936 (grades 3–8)	0.855–0.905 (grades 5 and 8, Biology I)	Not applicable	Not applicable	No
Delaware Delaware Student Testing Program	0.88–0.93 (grades 2–10)	0.91–0.93 (grades 2–10)	0.89–0.92 (grades 4, 6, 8, 11)	0.87–0.80 (grades 4, 6, 8, 11)	Interrater reliabilities: 0.59 and 0.65 (grades 3–11)	Yes in reading and math

SOURCES: CTB/McGraw-Hill (2009a, 2009b), Delaware Department of Education (2009), Human Resources Research Organization (2007a, 2007b), and Tennessee Department of Education (2010a).

NOTES: Estimates are expressed in Cronbach's alpha, unless otherwise noted. ECE = end-of-course examination.

[a] Uses stratified alphas, which combine internal consistency statistics for multiple-choice and constructed-response items.

they may have lower levels of reliability, on average, compared with the higher-stakes measures described in Table 4.1.

Promoting Reliability of Value-Added Estimates

We also looked for evidence of how these five systems are working to promote the reliability of their value-added estimates. We found that Hillsborough County plans to base teachers' evaluations on an average of three consecutive years of value-added estimates (Hillsborough County Public Schools, 2010). Similarly, Tennessee's teacher value-added reports show both single-year value-added estimates and, when available, a three-year average estimate. Also, in light of evidence that including multiple years of prior student achievement data increases the precision of teachers' effectiveness estimates (Ballou et al., 2004; Corcoran, 2010; McCaffrey et al., 2009), Tennessee attempts to include three to five years of students' prior achievement data in estimations of teachers' value added (SAS Institute, 2010; Tennessee Department of Education, n.d.-c).

Validity Considerations

We uncovered less evidence about how the profiled systems are assessing the validity of inferences they can draw about student performance. We did find that, because the grade 8 accountability assessment in Tennessee does not currently emphasize algebra, the TVAAS is reported to ensure that students who take Algebra I in grade 8 also take the state's Algebra I end-of-course assessment (DeLacy, 1999–2009).

As noted earlier, we also found that many of the locally developed tests in Hillsborough County included pretests as well as posttests associated with a particular course. If well developed, the pretests should provide baseline indicators of students' proficiency in the specific content covered by a given course. Thus, pretest scores may provide more-precise controls for students' prior knowledge of course content than do the students' other prior achievement measures in the content area. However, as noted earlier, it may still be desirable to include the other prior measures in value-added models in order to control more completely for students' prior achievement relative to their peers.

Vertical Scaling

Table 4.1 also illustrates that, in the five systems profiled here, only the state tests in Tennessee, Colorado, and Delaware attempt to use vertical scaling. In addition, we found that Colorado and Delaware use vertical scaling only in mathematics and reading (CTB/McGraw-Hill, 2009a; DeLacy, 1999–2009; Tennessee Department of Education, 2010a).

Measuring Growth in Nontested Subjects

The systems we profiled seemed to take one of several approaches to the use of student performance measures in teachers' evaluations. Hillsborough County proposes to use course-specific tests to estimate student growth in every grade and subject area. In a similar vein, Tennessee already tests students annually in four core subjects and is developing new end-of-course tests. However, Tennessee is also reportedly considering using schoolwide achievement growth to evaluate teachers in nontested subjects.

Denver and Washington, D.C., use different evaluation components for teachers in tested and nontested subjects and grades (see Tables 3.1 and 3.4), and they offer annual testing in fewer subjects than the other profiled systems. However, both Denver and D.C. hold teachers in tested and nontested grades equally accountable for schoolwide performance so that all teachers have equal incentives to collaborate with peers. Moreover, both Denver and D.C. allow teachers to choose their own student growth (or, in D.C., growth and performance level) targets on which they wish to demonstrate student learning. In both systems, teachers must set targets in consultation with their supervisors, and they are given parameters about the kinds of assessments they may choose from in a given grade and subject. Both districts place considerably less weight on these teacher-chosen measures than on value-added measures, a decision that seems reasonable, since the measures may vary among classrooms, making it difficult to gauge teachers' relative effectiveness. Still, this approach holds promise, particularly if school systems can increase the consistency of measures used among classrooms in a given subject and grade. It is important to note that Delaware, too, asks teachers to set at least one student learning goal each year in conjunction with an administrator, but, under the present iteration of DPAS II, there are no evaluation consequences if their students do not meet the goal (Delaware Department of Education, 2008a).

In addition, Delaware is reportedly considering the DIBELS and Gates-MacGinitie tests to assess reading skills in the early grades. How suitable are such measures for evaluating teachers? When administered in kindergarten, the DIBELS has been shown to be a useful predictor of students' risk for future reading difficulties (Elliott et al., 2001). However, because it is an oral reading test, it is important that teachers not test their own students if the test results are to be used in teachers' evaluations. Furthermore, it is important that testers be trained and periodically tested to ensure high interrater reliability. Gates-MacGinitie, in contrast, is administered via paper and pencil and is available for all grade levels, including early childhood, where it might serve as a useful measure in grades not covered by the state reading test. The third edition is reported to have internal consistency reliability coefficients of at least 0.9 in the early grades and above 0.8 in the upper grades (Missouri Department of Education, n.d.). Nevertheless, as noted earlier, measurement experts often express concerns about attaching high stakes to such diagnostic assessments as the DIBELS and Gates-MacGinitie because the assessments are designed to inform rather than evaluate instruction (see, for example, AERA, APA, & NCME, 1999).

Assigning Responsibility for Student Performance

We also reviewed documentation in the profiled systems to understand how they address complexities in assigning teachers responsibility for students in cases of partial-year enrollments, supplemental instruction, and team teaching.

In the case of students who transfer in to a teacher's class during the year and thus receive only a portion of their instruction from that teacher, the TVAAS has established that a student who is enrolled in a teacher's class for at least 150 days per year (or 75 days of a one-semester course) will have 100 percent of his or her test performance attributed to that teacher. Meanwhile, a student enrolled 75–149 days of the year will have 50 percent of his or her performance attributed to that teacher, and a student enrolled in a teacher's class fewer than 75 days of the school year will not have his or her performance attributed to that teacher (Tennessee Department of Education, n.d.-a). With regard to Denver, we found that Colorado's state test-based accountability system addresses student transfers somewhat similarly, in this case by excluding students from a value-added analysis who transfer into a teacher's class after October 1 of a given school year (Colorado Department of Education, 2008).

Regarding supplemental instruction and team teaching, however, it is not clear whether these two systems assign partial responsibility to each teaching team member or full responsibility to all teachers responsible for instructing a student in a particular subject that year. Tennessee's practice of assigning teachers partial responsibility for partial-year enrollments suggests that it may do the same for team teaching, but the documentation is not definitive on this point.

At the time this report was prepared, Hillsborough County had not determined how it would handle partial-year enrollments, supplemental teaching, or team teaching (Hillsborough County Public Schools, 2010). Staff from the D.C. IMPACT program told us that their forthcoming technical report, still being prepared, would describe procedures for partial-year enrollment and supplemental and team teaching. We did not find evidence of Delaware's policy considerations on this topic.

CHAPTER FIVE

Policy Recommendations and Conclusion

To help guide policymakers who wish to incorporate student achievement measures into teachers' evaluation systems, the following list of policy recommendations extracts central lessons from the preceding discussion:

- *Create comprehensive evaluation systems that incorporate multiple measures of teacher effectiveness.* The systems profiled in this report attest to the importance of evaluating teachers along multiple dimensions. These include not only value-added estimates of student achievement growth but also observational evidence of teacher effectiveness in the classroom and evidence of their professional contributions to their schools. Moreover, the examples remind us that evidence of classroom effectiveness includes the ability to plan appropriate lessons, set goals for student learning, and demonstrate that students have met those goals. The lesson is that teacher effectiveness is multifaceted, and no single measure of that effectiveness—whether observational or based on student test scores—is impervious to error. More-robust measures will therefore take multiple sources of evidence into account.

- *Attend not only to the technical properties of student assessments but also to how the assessments are being used in high-stakes contexts.* Technical reports are useful but do not provide all of the information policymakers need to ensure that their measures of student performance are robust. The reliability of scores and the validity of inferences drawn from those scores depend on how assessments are being used and the kinds of questions they are being used to answer. Policymakers therefore need to attend to how measures are being employed in their evaluation systems. This responsibility includes ensuring that teachers are not grading their own students on measures that carry high stakes; training and evaluating raters of open-ended assessments to encourage high levels of interrater reliability; and promoting consistent use and administration of student assessments across classrooms, particularly in the case of nonstandardized or noncommercial assessments, such as student writing prompts or portfolio assessments.

- *Promote consistency in the student performance measures teachers are allowed to choose.* If teachers of nontested subjects and grades are allowed to choose certain measures of student performance to include in their evaluations (as is now the case in Denver, D.C., and Delaware), provide clear parameters about the choices that are available. Where possible, guide teachers toward standardized assessments for which there is some documented evidence of usefulness for evaluating teachers' instructional practice. This is an instance where limiting the choices of measures available helps to promote consistency of measures across classrooms, resulting in measures of effectiveness that are comparable among teachers in the same subjects and grades.

- *Use multiple years of student achievement data in value-added estimation, and, where possible, average teachers' value-added estimates across multiple years.* Research has demonstrated that including multiple years of student achievement in teachers' value-added estimates leads to more-precise estimation of teachers' effectiveness (Ballou et al., 2004; McCaffrey et al., 2009). Such programs as the TVAAS therefore include up to five years of students' prior tests scores in their value-added estimation models insofar as such data are available (DeLacy, 1999–2009). In addition, research has shown that a considerable portion of the year-to-year variation in teachers' effectiveness estimates may be due to random error and that averaging across two to three years of estimates reduces this error (Goldhaber & Hansen, 2008; McCaffrey et al., 2009; Schochet & Chiang, 2010). Again, Tennessee serves as a model in that its teacher value-added reports present a teacher's single-year *and* three-year value-added estimate in each subject taught, insofar as the teacher has at least three years of value-added data on record.

- *Find ways to hold teachers accountable for students who are not included in their value-added estimates.* In the case of students who cannot reasonably be included in teachers' value-added estimates because they spent only a small part of the year in their current classroom, because they lack prior test scores, or for other reasons, teachers should be encouraged to demonstrate these students' progress in other ways. For example, having to show evidence of progress for these students on such measures as assignment completion and unit test performance may encourage teachers to attend to the needs of students whose test scores do not contribute to the teachers' value-added estimates.

Given the complexity of fairly incorporating student performance measures into teacher evaluation systems, experimentation is critical, and it is important for systems to learn from one another about what does and does not work. In the long term, it will also be important to examine how evaluation systems that incorporate student achievement and various rewards or sanctions affect the composition of the teacher workforce and the access of disadvantaged students to effective teachers. The hope is that by bringing teachers' evaluation scores into better alignment with their behavior and effectiveness, schools will have richer information with which to make a variety of personnel decisions, and teachers will have more-accurate information about how well their students are learning.

References

Aaronson, D., Barrow, L., & Sander, W. (2007). Teachers and student achievement in the Chicago Public High Schools. *Journal of Labor Economics, 25*, 95–135.

AERA, APA, & NCME. (1999). *Standards for educational and psychological testing.* Washington, DC: Author.

Associated Press. (2010, January 20). States change laws in hopes of Race to Top edge. *Education Week, 29.* Retrieved September 10, 2010, from http://www.edweek.org/ew/articles/2010/01/20/19rtt-sidebar.h29.html

Baker, E. L., Barton, P. E., Darling-Hammond, L., Haertel, E., Ladd, H. F., Linn, R. L., et al. (2010). *Problems with the use of student test scores to evaluate teachers* [Briefing Paper No. 278]. Washington, DC: Economic Policy Institute.

Ballou, D., Sanders, W., & Wright, P. (2004). Controlling for student background in value-added assessment of teachers. *Journal of Educational and Behavioral Statistics, 29*(1), 37–65.

Bill and Melinda Gates Foundation. (2010a). *Intensive partnerships for effective teaching.* Retrieved September 1, 2010, from http://www.gatesfoundation.org/united-states/Pages/statement-on-intensive-partnerships-effective-teaching.aspx

Bill and Melinda Gates Foundation. (2010b). *Measures of effective teaching (MET).* Retrieved April 5, 2010, from http://www.gatesfoundation.org/united-states/Pages/measures-of-effective-teaching-fact-sheet.aspx

Booher-Jennings, J. (2005). Below the bubble: "Educational triage" and the Texas Accountability System. *American Educational Research Journal, 42*(2), 231–268.

Buddin, R., McCaffrey, D. F., Kirby, S. N., & Xia, N. (2007). *Merit pay for Florida teachers: Design and implementation issues* [No. WR-508-FEA]. Santa Monica, CA: RAND Corporation. Retrieved November 2, 2010, from http://www.rand.org/pubs/working_papers/WR508/

Center for Educator Compensation Reform. (2007). *The evolution of performance pay in Florida.* Madison, WI: Author.

Chait, R., & Miller, R. T. (2010). *Treating different teachers differently: How state policy should act on differences in teacher performance to improve teacher effectiveness and equity.* Washington, DC: Center for American Progress.

Clotfelter, C. T., Ladd, H. F., & Vigdor, J. L. (2007a). *How and why do teacher credentials matter for student achievement?* [Working Paper No. 12828]. Washington, DC: National Center for Analysis of Longitudinal Data in Education Research.

Clotfelter, C. T., Ladd, H. F., & Vigdor, J. L. (2007b). Teacher-student matching and the assessment of teacher effectiveness. *Journal of Human Resources, 41*(4), 778–820.

Colorado Department of Education. (2008). *Colorado law pertaining to state assessments.* Retrieved September 26, 2010, from http://www.cde.state.co.us/cdeassess/co_law.html

Corcoran, S. (2010). *Can teachers be evaluated by their students' test scores? Should they be? The use of value-added measures of teacher effectiveness in policy and practice.* Providence, RI: Annenberg Institute for School Reform at Brown University.

Crocker, L., & Algina, J. (1986). *Introduction to classical and modern test theory.* Belmont, CA: Wadsworth Group, Thomson Learning, Inc.

CTB/McGraw-Hill. (2009a). *Colorado Student Assessment Program: Technical report, 2009.* Boulder, CO: Colorado Department of Education.

CTB/McGraw-Hill. (2009b). *Technical report for the Washington, DC Comprehensive Assessment System (DC CAS) spring 2009 administration.* Monterey, CA: Author.

DeGrow, B. (2007). *Denver's ProComp and teacher compensation reform in Colorado* (No. IP-5-2007). Golden, CO: Independence Institute. Retrieved October 25, 2010, from http://i2i.org/articles/IP_5_2007.pdf

DeLacy, M. (1999–2009). *Summary and comments on the studies produced by the Tennessee Value-Added Assessment System (TVAAS).* Retrieved September 27, 2010, from http://www.tagpdx.org/tvaas.htm

Delaware Department of Education. (2008a, August). *General questions asked from teachers and/or specialists.* Retrieved September 24, 2010, from http://www.doe.k12.de.us/csa/dpasii/files/DPASIIFrequentlyAskedQuestionsandAnswers7208.doc

Delaware Department of Education. (2008b). *Guide for teachers: DPAS II Delaware Performance Appraisal System.* Dover, DE: Author.

Delaware Department of Education. (2009). *Delaware Student Testing Program: Technical report—2008.* Dover, DE: Author.

Delaware Department of Education. (2010). *Matrix of appropriate measures of student growth for DPAS II Component V.* Retrieved September 23, 2010, from http://www.doe.k12.de.us/csa/dpasii/student_growth/files/Matrix_MeasDPASIIComp_V_June_Sum.doc

Denver Public Schools. (2006, November 28). *Student growth objectives: Career and technical education—High school teachers.* Retrieved October 13, 2010, from http://curriculum.dpsk12.org/psp/PostSecondary/cte/pdfs/StudentGrowth%20ObjHS-11-28-06.pdf

Denver Public Schools. (2008). *Professional evaluation handbook for teachers, student services professionals, student services professionals–itinerant, curriculum specialists, and evaluators.* Denver, CO: Author. Retrieved October 25, 2010, from http://static.dpsk12.org/gems/hr2009/HandbookCompProfEval08.pdf

Denver Public Schools. (2010a, July 12). *2010–11 ProComp payment opportunities.* Retrieved September 17, 2010, from http://static.dpsk12.org/gems/newprocomp/ProCompPaymentTable2010112010July12.xls

Denver Public Schools. (2010b). *Welcome to Teacher ProComp: Exceeds expectations.* Retrieved September 17, 2010, from http://denverprocomp.dpsk12.org/ExceedsExpectations#ExEx_E

Denver Public Schools. (2010c). *Welcome to Teacher ProComp: Overview.* Retrieved September 17, 2010, from http://denverprocomp.dpsk12.org/about/overview

District of Columbia Public Schools. (2009a). *IMPACT guidebooks.* Washington, DC: Author. Retrieved August 13, 2010, from http://www.dc.gov/DCPS/In+the+Classroom/Ensuring+Teacher+Success/IMPACT+(Performance+Assessment)/IMPACT+Guidebooks

District of Columbia Public Schools. (2009b). *IMPACT: The District of Columbia Public Schools effectiveness assessment system for school-based personnel: Group 1—General education teachers with individual value-added student achievement data.* Washington, DC: Author. Retrieved August 13, 2010, from http://www.dc.gov/DCPS/Files/downloads/TEACHING%20&%20LEARNING/IMPACT/IMPACT%20Guidebooks%202010-2011/DCPS-IMPACT-Group1-Guidebook-August-2010.pdf

District of Columbia Public Schools. (2009c). *IMPACT: The District of Columbia Public Schools effectiveness assessment system for school-based personnel: Group 2—General education teachers without individual value-added student achievement data*. Washington, DC: Author. Retrieved August 13, 2010, from http://www.dc.gov/DCPS/Files/downloads/TEACHING%20&%20LEARNING/IMPACT/IMPACT%20 Guidebooks%202010-2011/DCPS-IMPACT-Group2-Guidebook-August-2010.pdf

District of Columbia Public Schools. (2009d). *IMPACT: The District of Columbia Public Schools effectiveness assessment system for school-based personnel: Group 3—Special education teachers*. Washington, DC: Author. Retrieved August 13, 2010, from http://www.dc.gov/DCPS/Files/downloads/TEACHING%20&%20LEARNING/IMPACT/IMPACT%20 Guidebooks%202010-2011/DCPS-IMPACT-Group3-Guidebook-August-2010.pdf

District of Columbia Public Schools. (2010a). *IMPACTplus: The new performance-based compensation system for Washington Teachers' Union (WTU) members*. Retrieved September 14, 2010, from http://www.dc.gov/DCPS/In+the+Classroom/Ensuring+Teacher+Success/ IMPACT+(Performance+Assessment)/IMPACTplus

District of Columbia Public Schools. (2010b). *Teacher-assessed student achievement data (TAS) guidance*. Washington, DC: Author.

Elliott, J., Lee, S. W., & Tollefson, N. (2001). A reliability and validity study of the Dynamic Indicators of Basic Early Literacy Skills—Modified. *School Psychology Review, 30*(1), 33–49.

Ferguson, R. F., & Ladd, H. F. (1996). How and why money matters: An analysis of Alabama schools. In H. F. Ladd (Ed.), *Holding schools accountable: Performance-based education reform* (pp. 265–298). Washington, DC: The Brookings Institution.

Florida Department of Education. (2010). *Bureau of K–12 Assessment: End-of-course assessments*. Retrieved October 28, 2010, from http://fcat.fldoe.org/eoc/

Goldhaber, D. (2006). Everyone's doing it, but what does teacher testing tell us about teacher effectiveness? *Journal of Human Resources, 42*(4), 765–794.

Goldhaber, D. (2010). *When the stakes are high, can we rely on value-added? Exploring the use of value-added models to inform teacher workforce decisions*. Washington, DC: Center for American Progress.

Goldhaber, D., & Hansen, M. (2008). *Is it just a bad class? Assessing the stability of measured teacher performance* [No. 5]. Bothell, WA: Center on Reinventing Public Education.

Gordon, R., Kane, T. J., & Staiger, D. O. (2006). *Identifying effective teachers using performance on the job*. Washington, DC: The Brookings Institution.

Hamilton, L. S., Stecher, B. M., Marsh, J. A., McCombs, J. S., Robyn, A., Russell, J., Naftel, S., & Barney, H. (2007). *Implementing standards-based accountability under No Child Left Behind: Responses of superintendents, principals, and teachers in three states* [No. MG-589-NSF]. Santa Monica, CA: RAND Corporation. Retrieved November 2, 2010, from http://www.rand.org/pubs/monographs/MG589/

Harris, D. N., & Sass, T. R. (2008). *Teacher training, teacher quality, and student achievement* [Working Paper No. 3]. Washington, DC: National Center for Analysis of Longitudinal Data in Education Research.

Hershberg, T. (2005). Value-added assessment and systemic reform: A response to the challenge of human capital development. *Phi Delta Kappan, 87*(4), 276–283.

Hill, H. C., Rowan, B., & Ball, D. L. (2005). Effects of teachers' mathematical knowledge for teaching on student achievement. *American Educational Research Journal, 42*(2), 371–406.

Hillsborough County Public Schools. (2010). *Empowering teachers: Student learning gains questions*. Retrieved September 21, 2010, from http://communication.sdhc.k12.fl.us/empoweringteachers/?page_id=317

Houston Independent School District. (2010). *ASPIRE: Value-added frequently asked questions*. Retrieved September 27, 2010, from http://portal.battelleforkids.org/Aspire/Value-Added/FAQs.html?sflang=en

Human Resources Research Organization. (2007a). *Florida Comprehensive Assessment Test (FCAT) Reading and Mathematics: Technical report for 2006 test administrations*. San Antonio, TX: Harcourt Assessment, Inc. Retrieved September 28, 2010, from http://fcat.fldoe.org/pdf/2006FCATWritingPlus-tech-Report.pdf

Human Resources Research Organization. (2007b). *Florida Comprehensive Assessment Test (FCAT) Writing: Technical report for 2006 test administration*. San Antonio, TX: Harcourt Assessment, Inc. Retrieved September 28, 2010, from http://fcat.fldoe.org/pdf/2006FCATWritingPlus-tech-Report.pdf

Klein, S. P., McCaffrey, D. F., Stecher, B. M., & Koretz, D. (1995). The reliability of mathematics portfolio scores: Lessons from the Vermont experience. *Applied Measurement in Education, 8*(3), 243–260.

Koretz, D. M. (2008). *Measuring up: What educational testing really tells us.* Cambridge, MA: Harvard University Press.

Koretz, D. M., & Barron, S. (1998). *The validity of gains in scores on the Kentucky Instructional Results Information System (KIRIS)* [No. MR-1014-EDU]. Santa Monica, CA: RAND Corporation. Retrieved November 2, 2010, from http://www.rand.org/pubs/monograph_reports/MR1014/

Koretz, D. M., & Hamilton, L. S. (2006). Testing for accountability in K–12. In R. L. Brennan (Ed.), *Educational measurement* (Fourth ed., pp. 531–578). Westport, CT: Praeger.

Lankford, H., Boyd, D., Loeb, S., & Wyckoff, J. (2010, November 6). *Measuring test measurement error: A general approach and policy implications.* Paper presented at the Association of Public Policy Analysis and Management Fall Conference, Boston, MA.

LeMahieu, P. G., Gitomer, D. H., & Eresh, J. T. (1995). Portfolios in large-scale assessment: Difficult but not impossible. *Educational Measurement: Issues and Practice, 14*(3), 11–16, 25–28.

Locker, R. (2010, January 15). Tennessee lawmakers approve teacher evaluation plan. *The Commercial Appeal, Memphis, Tennessee.* Retrieved September 28, 2010, from http://www.commercialappeal.com/news/2010/jan/15/tennessee-senate-passes-teacher-evaluation-bill/

Martineau, J. A. (2006). Distorting value added: The use of longitudinal, vertically scaled student achievement data for growth-based, value-added accountability. *Educational Measurement: Issues and Practice, 31*(1), 35–62.

McCaffrey, D. F., Lockwood, J. R., Koretz, D. M., & Hamilton, L. S. (2003). *Evaluating value-added models for teacher accountability* [No. MG-158-EDU]. Santa Monica, CA: RAND Corporation. Retrieved November 2, 2010, from http://www.rand.org/pubs/monographs/MG158/

McCaffrey, D. F., Sass, T. R., Lockwood, J. R., & Mihaly, K. (2009). The intertemporal variability of teacher effect estimates. *Education Finance and Policy, 4*(4), 572–606.

Missouri Department of Education. (n.d.). *Reading assessment instruments.* Retrieved September 29, 2010, from http://dese.mo.gov/divimprove/curriculum/commarts/readassess.pdf

Mitchell, N. (2005, December 29). Denver teachers opt for merit pay. *Rocky Mountain News.*

National Center on Performance Incentives. (2008). *State-by-state resources: State initiatives overview.* Nashville, TN: Author.

National Comprehensive Center for Teacher Quality. (2010). *Guide to teacher evaluation products.* Retrieved August 10, 2010, from http://www3.learningpt.org/tqsource/gep/default.aspx

Odden, A., & Kelley, C. (2002). *Paying teachers for what they know and do: New and smarter compensation strategies to improve schools* (2nd ed.). Thousand Oaks, CA: Corwin Press.

Perie, M., Gong, B., Marion, S., & Wurtzel, J. (2007). *The role of interim assessments in a comprehensive assessment system: A policy brief.* Dover, NH: National Center for the Improvement of Educational Assessment.

Prince, C. D., Schuermann, P. J., Guthrie, J. W., Witham, P. J., Milanowski, A. T., & Thorn, C. A. (2009). *The other 69 percent: Fairly rewarding the performance of teachers of nontested subjects and grades.* Washington, DC: Center for Educator Compensation Reform.

Rivkin, S. G., Hanushek, E. A., & Kain, J. F. (2005). Teachers, schools, and academic achievement. *Econometrica, 73*(2), 417–458.

Rockoff, J. E. (2004). The impact of individual teachers on student achievement: Evidence from panel data. *American Economic Review, 94*(2), 247–252.

Rothstein, J. (2010). Teacher quality in educational production: Tracking, decay, and student achievement. *Quarterly Journal of Economics, 125*(1), 175–214.

Sanders, W. L., & Horn, S. P. (1998). Research findings from the Tennessee Value-Added Assessment System (TVAAS) database: Implications for educational evaluation and research. *Journal of Personnel Evaluation in Education, 12*(3), 247–256.

Sanders, W. L., & Rivers, J. (1996). *Research progress report: Cumulative and residual effects of teachers on future student academic achievement: Tennessee Value-Added Assessment System.* Knoxville, TN: University of Tennessee Value-Added Research and Assessment Center.

SAS Institute. (2010). *SAS® EVAAS® for K–12.* Retrieved September 26, 2010, from http://www.sas.com/govedu/edu/k12/evaas/index.html

Schmidt, W. H., Houang, R. T., & McKnight, C. C. (2005). Value-added research: Right idea but wrong solution? In R. Lissitz (Ed.), *Value-added models in education: Theory and applications* (pp. 145–165). Maple Grove, MN: JAM Press.

Schochet, P. Z., & Chiang, H. S. (2010). *Error rates in measuring teacher and school performance based on student test score gains* [No. NCEE 2010-4004]. Washington, DC: National Center for Education Evaluation and Regional Assistance, Institute of Education Sciences, U.S. Department of Education.

School District of Hillsborough County. (2007). *Florida End of Course Exam (ECE) Clearinghouse.* Retrieved September 25, 2010, from http://is4.sdhc.k12.fl.us/ece/doclist.html

Stecher, B. M., Epstein, S., Hamilton, L. S., Marsh, J. A., Robyn, A., McCombs, J. S., Russell, J., & Naftel, S. (2008). *Pain and gain: Implementing No Child Left Behind in three states, 2004–2006* [No. MG-784-NSF]. Santa Monica, CA: RAND Corporation. Retrieved November 2, 2010, from http://www.rand.org/pubs/monographs/MG784/

Summers, A., & Wolfe, B. (1977). Do schools make a difference? *American Economic Review, 67*(4), 639–652.

Tennessee Department of Education. (n.d.-a). *Faculty/student linkage for teacher effect.* Nashville, TN: Author.

Tennessee Department of Education. (n.d.-b). *Framework for evaluation and professional growth.* Retrieved September 25, 2010, from http://state.tn.us/education/frameval/

Tennessee Department of Education. (n.d.-c). *TVAAS: Tennessee Value-Added Assessment System fact sheet—assessment literacy training.* Retrieved September 24, 2010, from http://www.tn.gov/education/assessment/doc/TVAAS_Fact_Sheet.pdf

Tennessee Department of Education. (2010a). *Secondary assessments.* Retrieved September 25, 2010, from http://www.state.tn.us/education/assessment/secondary.shtml

Tennessee Department of Education. (2010b). *Achievement test.* Retrieved September 25, 2010, from http://www.state.tn.us/education/assessment/achievement.shtml

Texas Education Agency and Pearson. (2010). *Technical digest 2008–2009.* Austin, TX: Texas Education Agency. Retrieved September 27, 2010, from http://www.tea.state.tx.us/index3.aspx?id=2147484418&menu_id=793

Toch, T., & Rothman, R. (2008). *Rush to judgment: Teacher evaluation in public education.* Washington, DC: Education Sector.

Tucker, P. D. (1997). Lake Wobegon: Where all teachers are competent (or, have we come to terms with the problem of incompetent teachers?). *Journal of Personnel Evaluation in Education, 11,* 103–126.

U.S. Department of Education. (2010). *Teacher Incentive Fund—Awards.* Retrieved September 23, 2010, from http://www2.ed.gov/programs/teacherincentive/awards.html

Vigdor, J. L. (2008). Scrap the sacrosanct salary schedule. *Education Next, 8*(4), 36–42.

Weisberg, D., Sexton, S., Mulhern, J., & Keeling, D. (2009). *The widget effect: Our national failure to acknowledge and act on differences in teacher effectiveness.* New York: The New Teacher Project.

Zelinski, A. (2010, July 9). *Teacher evaluation panel hashes out first set of recommendations.* Retrieved September 20, 2010, from http://www.tnreport.com/2010/07/teacher-evaluation-panel-hashes-out-first-set-of-recommendations/

About the Authors

Jennifer L. Steele is an associate policy researcher at the RAND Corporation in Washington, D.C., where she studies education policy, education-based labor market incentives, and data-driven decisionmaking in schools. She is currently examining the policies and practices of charter and traditional schools in New Orleans and studying changes in the distribution of teacher quality in response to incentives in four urban districts. Her recent work includes estimating the impact of higher education incentives on the distribution of academically talented teachers in California. Dr. Steele's research has appeared in such publications as the *Journal of Research on Educational Effectiveness*, the *Journal of Policy Analysis and Management*, and *The Future of Children*. She holds an Ed.D. in administration, planning, and social policy from Harvard University.

Laura S. Hamilton is a senior behavioral scientist at the RAND Corporation and an adjunct associate professor in the University of Pittsburgh's Learning Sciences and Policy program. Her research focuses on educational assessment, accountability, and the measurement of instruction and leadership practices. She has directed several large studies, including a study of teachers' and principals' responses to state standards-based accountability policies and an evaluation of a performance-based compensation system for principals. She has served on a number of national panels, including the American Psychological Association/American Educational Research Association/National Council on Measurement in Education Joint Committee to Revise the *Standards for Educational and Psychological Testing*, the Center on Education Policy's Panel on High School Exit Examinations and Panel on Student Achievement Under No Child Left Behind, the Brookings National Commission on Choice in K–12 Education, and the technical advisory group for a national study of charter management organizations. She received a Ph.D. in educational psychology and an M.S. in statistics from Stanford University.

Brian M. Stecher is a senior social scientist and acting director of the RAND Education program. His research focuses on measuring educational quality and evaluating education reforms, particularly assessment and accountability systems. During his 20 years at RAND, he has directed prominent national and state evaluations, including studies of No Child Left Behind, the Empowering Effective Teachers program of the Gates Foundation, mathematics and science systemic reforms, and class-size reduction. His measurement-related expertise includes test development, test validation, and the use of assessments for school improvement. Dr. Stecher has served on expert panels relating to standards, assessments, and accountability for the National Academies, and he is currently a member of the National Academy of Sciences Board on Testing and Assessment. He holds a Ph.D. in education from the University of California, Los Angeles.